RIVER MONSTERS
GIANT BARBS

BY JOANNE MATTERN

BELLWETHER MEDIA • MINNEAPOLIS, MN

EPIC

EPIC

EPIC BOOKS are no ordinary books. They burst with intense action, high-speed heroics, and shadows of the unknown. Are you ready for an Epic adventure?

This edition first published in 2024 by Bellwether Media, Inc.

No part of this publication may be reproduced in whole or in part without written permission of the publisher. For information regarding permission, write to Bellwether Media, Inc., Attention: Permissions Department, 6012 Blue Circle Drive, Minnetonka, MN 55343.

Library of Congress Cataloging-in-Publication Data

LC record for Giant Barbs available at: https://lccn.loc.gov/2023040018

Text copyright © 2024 by Bellwether Media, Inc. EPIC and associated logos are trademarks and/or registered trademarks of Bellwether Media, Inc.

Editor: Elizabeth Neuenfeldt   Designer: Josh Brink

Printed in the United States of America, North Mankato, MN.

TABLE OF CONTENTS

MEET THE KING	4
WATER GIANT	6
LIVING LARGE	12
BIG DANGERS	18
GLOSSARY	22
TO LEARN MORE	23
INDEX	24

MEET THE KING

Giant barbs are among the world's largest **freshwater** fish. People call them the "king of fish!"

These fish live in rivers within Southeast Asia. Sometimes they swim in **canals** or flooded areas.

CANAL

ANOTHER NAME

Giant barbs are also called Siamese carps.

GIANT BARB RANGE

RANGE =

WATER GIANT

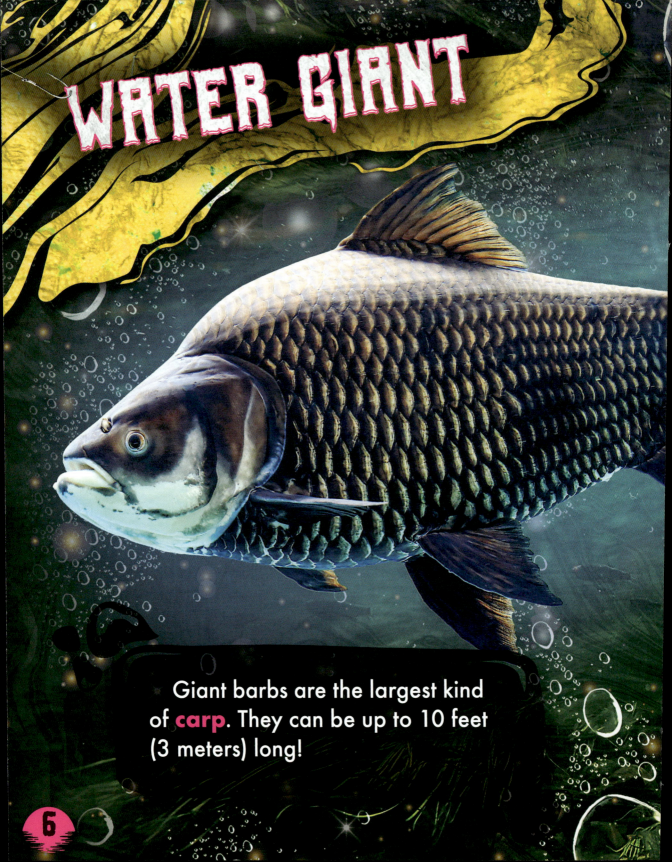

Giant barbs are the largest kind of **carp**. They can be up to 10 feet (3 meters) long!

These fish can weigh around 660 pounds (299 kilograms).

SIZE COMPARISON

AVERAGE ADULT MAN
Height: 5.75 feet (1.75 meters)
Weight: 200 pounds (91 kilograms)

GIANT BARB
Length: up to 10 feet (3 meters)
Weight: around 660 pounds (299 kilograms)

Giant barbs are mostly black and gray. The bottoms of their bodies can be yellow or brown.

They are covered with big **scales**. Their scales can be as big as the palm of a person's hand!

SCALES

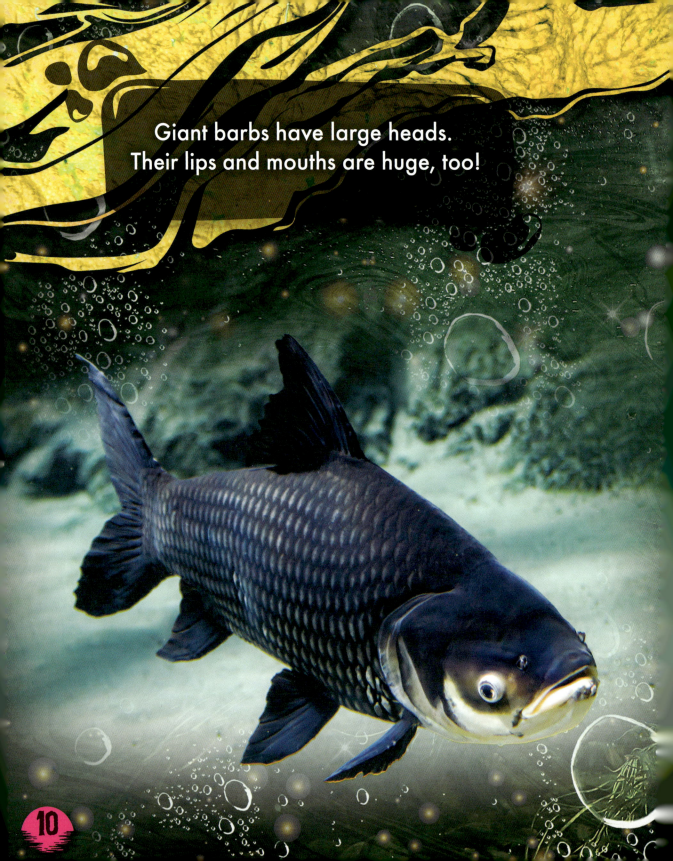

Giant barbs have large heads. Their lips and mouths are huge, too!

IDENTIFY A GIANT BARB

BLACK AND GRAY BODY

LARGE HEAD

BIG LIPS

HUGE MOUTH

GIANT BARB SUCKING UP WATER

They use their mouths to suck food out of the water.

LIVING LARGE

Giant barbs mostly eat **plankton** and **algae**. They also eat seaweed.

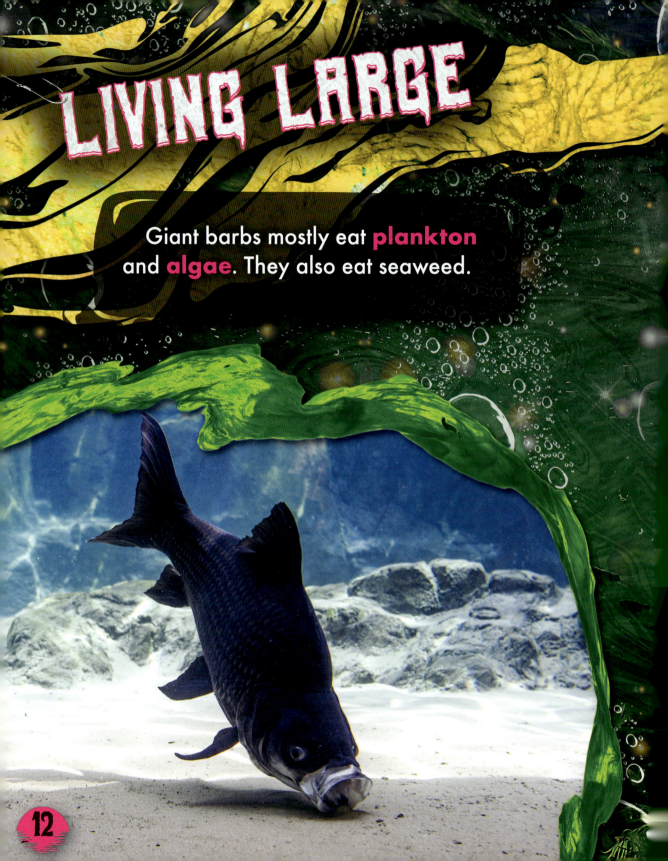

If rivers flood, they will eat land plants and fruits under the water.

Giant barbs swim slowly in rivers. They usually live in pairs.

These fish **migrate** to find food. They will swim to ponds, canals, and flooded forests. They can **adapt** to different freshwater **habitats**!

It is not certain how giant barbs lay their eggs. They may **spawn** in flooded areas.

Young barbs can be found in swamps and canals.

FLOODED AREA

BIG MAMA

Large female giant barbs can make more than 10 million eggs!

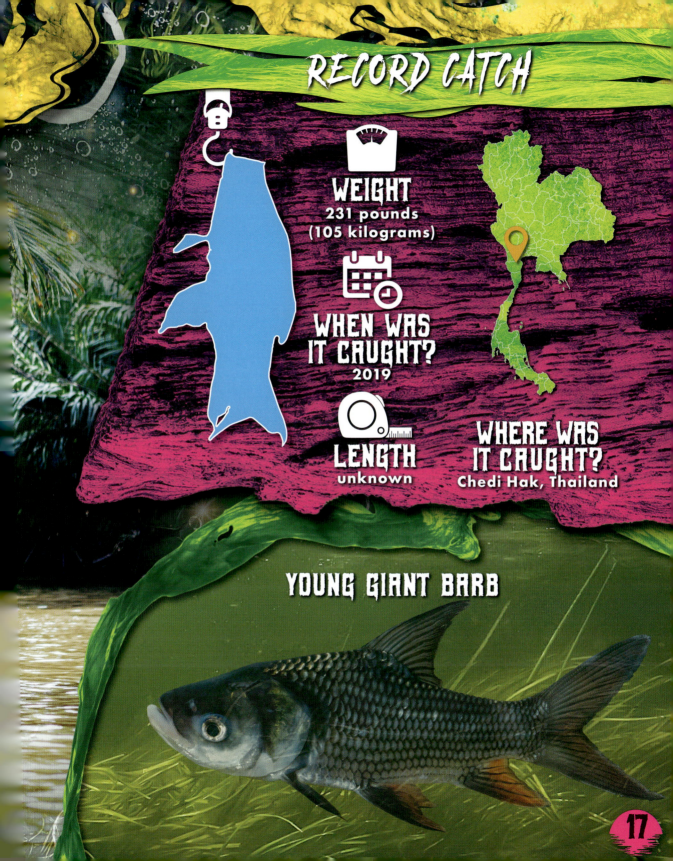

RECORD CATCH

WEIGHT
231 pounds
(105 kilograms)

WHEN WAS IT CAUGHT?
2019

LENGTH
unknown

WHERE WAS IT CAUGHT?
Chedi Hak, Thailand

YOUNG GIANT BARB

BIG DANGERS

Giant barbs are **critically endangered**. The biggest threat to them is **overfishing**. Many barbs are caught before they can become adults.

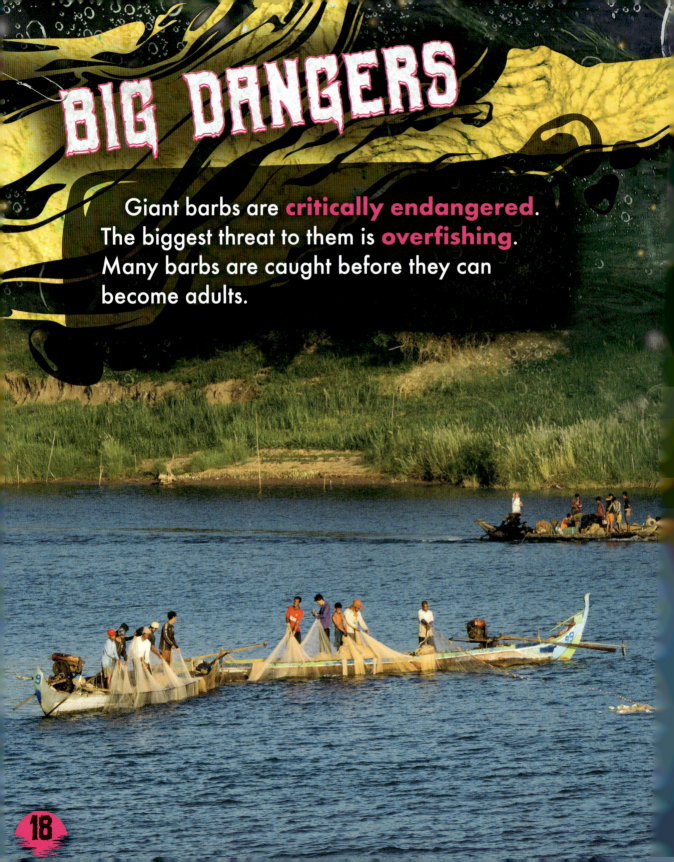

They are losing their habitats, too. Dams have stopped these fish from migrating. They cannot get food.

DAM

People are helping giant barbs. Governments have made it illegal to catch and sell giant barbs. People also raise giant barbs on fish farms.

GIANT BARB STATS

| LEAST CONCERN | NEAR THREATENED | VULNERABLE | ENDANGERED | CRITICALLY ENDANGERED | EXTINCT IN THE WILD | EXTINCT |

LIFE SPAN
unknown

THREATS
habitat loss, overfishing

WHAT AN HONOR!

Cambodia named the giant barb its national fish in 2005.

This work will help giant barbs remain the "king of fish!"

GLOSSARY

adapt—to change to fit different conditions

algae—plants and plantlike living things; most kinds of algae grow in water.

canals—waterways built by people

carp—a kind of large Asian freshwater fish that is often raised for food

critically endangered—greatly in danger of dying out

freshwater—related to water that is not salty

habitats—places where animals live

migrate—to move from one place to another, often with the seasons

overfishing—using up the number of fish by fishing too much

plankton—tiny plants and animals that live in water

scales—small plates that cover the bodies of some fish

spawn—to lay eggs

TO LEARN MORE

AT THE LIBRARY

Forest, Christopher. *Fish*. Minneapolis, Minn.: Abdo Publishing, 2021.

Mattern, Joanne. *Mekong Giant Catfish*. Minneapolis, Minn.: Bellwether Media, 2024.

Teckentrup, Britta. *Fish Everywhere*. Somerville, Mass.: Candlewick Press, 2019.

ON THE WEB

FACTSURFER

Factsurfer.com gives you a safe, fun way to find more information.

1. Go to www.factsurfer.com.

2. Enter "giant barbs" into the search box and click 🔍.

3. Select your book cover to see a list of related content.

INDEX

adults, 18
Cambodia, 21
canals, 4, 15, 16
carp, 6
colors, 8
critically endangered, 18
dams, 19
eggs, 16
farms, 20
females, 16
flooded areas, 4, 13, 15, 16
food, 11, 12, 13, 15, 19
governments, 20
habitats, 15, 19
heads, 10
identify, 11
lips, 10

migrate, 15, 19
mouths, 10, 11
name, 4, 5
overfishing, 18
pairs, 14
people, 20
ponds, 15
range, 4, 5
record catch, 17
rivers, 4, 13, 14
scales, 9
size, 4, 6, 7, 9, 10, 16
Southeast Asia, 4
spawn, 16
stats, 21
swamps, 16
young, 16, 17

The images in this book are reproduced through the courtesy of: Danny Ye, cover (hero), pp. 10-11; Rocksweeper, pp. 2-3, 22-23, 24 (background); p.Lightning, p. 4; Yuttana Joe, p. 4 (canal); Jürgen & Christine Sohns, pp. 6-7; Tanteckken, p. 8; Stbernardstudio, pp. 8-9, 13; Moo traforthree, p. 9 (scales); Eliana Abraham, p. 11 (black and gray body, huge mouth); Anton Watman, p. 11 (large head); Morrissey Design Studio, p. 11 (big lips); Chat9780, p. 11; Tony Anwar, p. 12; tristan tan, p. 14; Cheng Wei, p. 15; ArtRomanov, pp. 16-17; Tinakorn Suksapsri, p. 17; Michael Greenfelder/ Alamy, pp. 18-19; Sarawut Sangsala, p. 19; bigjom, p. 20.